C000131403

THE
EMPOWERMENT
POCKETBOOK

By Mike Applegarth & Keith Posner
Drawings by Phil Hailstone

"Empowerment allows an organisation to unlock the hidden potential in its workforce. This pocketbook will assist anyone who wants to learn about empowerment, what differentiates it from delegation, and how it can be implemented in the work place."
Adrian Guttridge, Manager, Andersen Consulting

"I particularly liked the way the authors have used everyday comparisons, such as driving a car, to explain their approach to the subject. Individual pages could be used as presentation material or workshop handouts."
Bob Owen, Branch Manager, Cornhill Insurance

CONTENTS

Who is this book for?

This book is not just for managers; it is also relevant to trainers, consultants and key staff from personnel/human resources departments who are interested in getting the best from their workforce. Moreover, it will interest employees who want to learn more about how to be empowered.

'Empowerment' may not be a new concept to you, but these pages will help clarify the subject and will demonstrate how to overcome the problems many organisations experience because they '**talked about it and around it**' but didn't know how to '**live it**'.

It is still too common for 'delegation' and 'empowerment' to be confused, and for the latter to be regarded as something you can use over somebody else, like having authority.

Read on and discover what 'empowerment' is and what can be gained when it's in place, how to put it there and keep it there. Whether at local, department or team level, or within the organisation as a whole, 'empowerment' could make that all important difference.

INTRODUCTION

A verse reaction

It's the word that we've all heard, but just what does it mean? Like Father Christmas and the Dodo bird, it's talked of but never seen.

'Empowerment', 'Synergy' - impressive words, particularly in Scrabble. Yet without a clue how to see them through, they're merely psychobabble.

For the manager they're heaven-sent, evoking freedom and good intent: employees, though, think 'What's the fuss? They've still no idea how to manage us'.

'They don't give us goals and make clear the scope, they build the gibbet and hand out the rope.'

'We're never developed, it's just more of the same, there simply aren't the hours.'

Still, the only culture where no one gets blamed, is the one where it really empowers!

WHAT IS EMPOWERMENT?

EMPOWERMENT: THE DEFINITION

EMPOWERMENT: THE DEFINITION

Most dictionaries cite the first two words listed below but not the third, which could explain why it's never been applied properly:

Authority; Power; Licence

Only the third word provides the foundation for successful implementation in organisations, because:

- **Authority** only exists where you have subordinates

- **Power** can be switched on and off

- **Licence** defines the scope and conditions which apply to an activity, and is issued after those concerned have proven their ability

WHAT IS EMPOWERMENT?

TO LICENSE IS TO EMPOWER

If we take the example of a **Car Driver's Licence**, it becomes easier to relate the definition to the practice of empowerment:

- The licence empowers you to drive a car on the country's roads once ability is proven

- The conditions are not so restrictive that the car must be a specific model, or that the route must always be the same

- However, it does not empower you to drive a heavy goods vehicle (HGV) or a fire-engine for which separate licences are required

- The Highway Code provides guidelines of acceptability with which every driver should be familiar

- The outcome is the same for all - arrival at our destinations safely

WHAT IS EMPOWERMENT?

TO LICENSE IS TO EMPOWER

What the driver's example means at work:

- Empowers employees to act within an organisational framework without frequent recourse to authority

- Employees focus on outcomes and are not constrained by rigid controls - they are involved at the planning stage

- Authority may still need to be sought outside the scope of the empowerment, or further development provided

- Codes of Practice, a Statement of Values or Customer Charters can still exist as core outcomes

- Everyone has the freedom to achieve using their initiative

WHAT IS EMPOWERMENT?

3 STATES OF EMPOWERMENT

In any team or organisational framework people are either:

- **Empowered**   where they have the freedom to act within known boundaries to achieve agreed outcomes

- **Disempowered**   where the freedom they once enjoyed has been taken away

- **Unempowered**   where the freedom has never been granted in the first place or where they are not aware it exists

Put more simply, at work we either feel **spurred** - in other words, empowered - or we feel **spurned** - which is either disempowered or unempowered.

WHAT DOES EMPOWERMENT LOOK LIKE?

In all the organisations where we've assisted in establishing an 'empowered' culture, it was easier for employees to identify with 'non-empowerment'.

You may find the next page helpful in prompting a discussion on what empowerment may mean to your organisation. As a manager, you could use it as part of a team-meeting to address staff development. As a trainer, use it during a programme on communication issues or management development.

You will need to be prepared with your own responses too.

Ask the group when they last felt **empowered, unempowered** or **disempowered,** and get them to describe the nature of those feelings.

WHAT IS EMPOWERMENT?

QUESTIONS TO CONSIDER

Consider these three questions:

1. What is your definition of empowerment?
2. What are some examples of empowerment?
3. What are examples of a lack of empowerment?

Without discussion with others in your group, write down your own answers to these questions and try to finish in ten minutes.

1. My definition of empowerment is: _____

_____

2. Examples of   A _____
   empowerment are: B _____
                     C _____

3. Examples of a lack   A _____
   of empowerment are: B _____
                        C _____

Now discuss your responses with those of your group and arrive at a group definition and at least five examples for questions 2 and 3.

WHAT IS EMPOWERMENT?

CLARIFYING THE PICTURE

When arriving at examples of empowerment
or lack of empowerment, ask your group
to describe:

- What they saw
- What they heard
- How they felt

Fairly soon you will have a clear
picture of what empowerment
should look like with that
group of people.

EMPOWERMENT V DELEGATION

Empowerment is not delegation because:

- **Empowerment** is where the organisation has enabled or coached the employee and now continues to support that person within the scope of his or her own work, as previously agreed

- **Delegation** is about giving away parts of your own job to someone else; it is not about giving people scope within their own jobs

However, the processes involved in **delegating** should be similar to those for **empowering**.

With empowerment, accountability and responsibility rest with the person empowered. With delegation, responsibility can be passed on but accountability for ensuring the work is done stays with the person who delegated the task.

WHAT IS EMPOWERMENT?

OUTCOMES NOT INPUTS

Empowerment means clarifying required outcomes, not dictating inputs. Take, for example, the activity of changing a car wheel. By focusing on the **outcomes** rather than the process, there is scope for initiative and for attaining a sense of accomplishment:

- The spare wheel is securely fitted and complies with Ministry of Transport (MoT) requirements
- The damaged wheel and tools used are securely stowed in their allocated place
- The car has suffered no damage as a consequence of changing the wheel
- You suffer no injury as a result of changing the wheel
- No damage or suffering is caused to other road users whilst changing the wheel
- You arrive safely at your destination no later than twenty minutes beyond any pre-arranged appointment time

The above describes what the activity should look like when it has been properly completed. It does not tell you how to do it. People can be empowered to achieve the results with scope to think for themselves.

OUTCOMES NOT INPUTS

Contrast the outcomes shown on the previous page with the **process** for changing a car wheel below:

1. Stop the car and park where you can get access to the wheels and the boot without posing a danger for other road users or yourself
2. Identify the damaged tyre
3. Remove the spare wheel from its allocated place along with the jack and wheel brace
4. Use the wheel brace to remove the hub cap on the damaged wheel and to loosen the wheel nuts **without removing them**
5. Locate the jack at its nearest jacking point to the damaged wheel and use it to raise the car off the ground, allowing clearance for a fully inflated wheel

CONTINUED

OUTCOMES NOT INPUTS

6   Remove the damaged wheel and replace it with the spare

7   Tighten the wheel nuts in a sequence of opposites rather than clockwise or anti-clockwise

8   Use the jack to lower the car, then remove it

9   Re-tighten the wheel nuts

10 Replace the hub cap

11 Put the damaged wheel where the spare was and the tools back in their allocated place

12 As soon as possible, get the damaged wheel repaired and check the inflation of your tyres

So, what are the differences?

WHAT IS EMPOWERMENT?

OUTCOMES NOT INPUTS
DIFFERENCES BETWEEN THE TWO

Inputs	Outcomes
Directives	Achievements
Tasks	Measurable goals
Processes	What the job looks like when it's done well!
Resources - people	Signposts
- money	
- time	Significant indicators which reflect desired performance
- equipment	
- materials	
The means to the end	The end-result
Don't always address 'what ifs' (What if there's no jack or the wheel nuts are too tight to remove?)	Scope for initiative, directed towards outcomes
What the unempowering manager expresses	**What the empowering manager clarifies and monitors against**

EXPLORING THE NEED

THE BENEFITS OF EMPOWERMENT

Just as car drivers feel free to make their own decisions about how to arrive at a particular destination, so empowered employees also feel less constrained:

Benefits to the driver

- ✔ No fixed (bus) routes
- ✔ No unnecessary waiting
  (at bus stops or train stations)
- ✔ No longer a passenger
  (but in control)
- ✔ Driver puts in the effort to arrive
  rather than letting someone else
- ✔ Driver explores the possibilities of
  quicker, easier journeys and ways
  of up-grading the quality (of the car)

Benefits to the employee

- ✔ No strict operational procedures
- ✔ Just Do It (JDI) - no constant recourse
  for approval
- ✔ Not having to await instructions as you
  create your own work plan
- ✔ Self-motivation - you accept
  responsibility for your own destiny
- ✔ Practices are reviewed more frequently
  and creativity and initiative flourish

BENEFITS TO THE ORGANISATION

When it comes down to it, nobody does anything because it helps the organisation; they do it because there's something in it for them. At least empowerment is one of those initiatives that reaps benefits for the individual first whilst enhancing the organisation, because:

✔ The workforce will discover ways to enhance efficiency and quality through the natural course of their work

✔ Everyone is clear about the direction they're heading in so there is less duplication of effort, if at all

✔ Staff are enabled before being empowered so fewer mistakes are likely

✔ Wastage of resources is easily identified and eliminated

✔ Employees share more in the 'mission' and are therefore prepared to give that little bit extra to achieve it (more for less)

✔ Money that would otherwise have been spent on incentive schemes can be invested in training/enabling with longer-term gains for the organisation

Of course, all the above will only exist if empowerment is implemented correctly and with total commitment. More on that in a later chapter.

SYMPTOMS TO LOOK FOR

Does your organisation, or part of it, show any of the following symptoms?

- ✘ Staff are unproductive much of the time
- ✘ Everyone appears to be busy, but not a lot seems to be achieved
- ✘ Staff don't criticise the way things are done
- ✘ Ideas or inputs from subordinates are not forthcoming
- ✘ Staff are constantly being reprimanded for either acting without authority or not showing initiative
- ✘ Staff turnover is increasing
- ✘ Customers are dissatisfied with particular aspects of service
- ✘ Employees know what their jobs are, but they don't know what is expected of them
- ✘ The finger of blame always has to point at someone
- ✘ The left hand doesn't know what the right hand is doing
- ✘ Management spends too much time doing other workers' tasks instead of managing
- ✘ An acute absence of creativity and initiative

If you answer 'yes' to any of the above, then empowerment might hold the solution.

ADDRESSING THE SYMPTOMS

Finding the right question to ask will make all the difference to whether you find the right solution.

All the symptoms on the previous page can prompt the following questions:

- Why is this happening?
- How can I prevent it from happening again?
- What will it look like when things are done well?

Establishing 'why it is happening' will heighten your awareness; finding the answer to 'prevent it recurring' might put you in a better position to take control of the situation. However, if you stop there you could be regarded as **reactive**, and would forever be behind yourself.

Organisations which ask 'what it will look like when things are done well' are the ones which are **proactive** and, therefore, better able to bring about the outcomes they seek. They spend more time looking ahead and getting there than they spend trying to change the past, whilst losing touch with the future.

THE EMPOWERER'S NEED

Those empowering will need training in how to clarify desired outcomes and how to identify what empowered staff should at least be capable of. In particular, they will need guidance to help them avoid:

- Rescinding the empowerment when it suits them

- Changing the terms of the licence without prior consultation with those affected

- Chastising those who achieve results, because they didn't do it their way

- Taking over the work themselves, or persistently dictating how it should be done

- Looking for people to blame, instead of lessons to be learned, when things go wrong

- Requesting that their approval is sought before the employee's initiative is implemented

- Telling staff what the plan is, without having involved them in it

- Giving no guidance or outcomes and just dumping tasks on employees

- Keeping a 'closed-door and ignore' policy towards the team

DISEMPOWERING

How can empowerment be taken away? The driver's licence provides a useful analogy once again:

- There must be evidence of breach of the terms of the licence
- The offender must be told how and when the breach occurred
- The offender will have known the consequences of the offence before committing it
- **There should be no surprises**, but allowance should be made for different driving styles
- However, one person's offence does not remove the licence for everyone

(23)

WHERE EMPOWERMENT MAY NOT APPLY

Some organisations, or at least parts of organisations, may not consider it appropriate to empower the workforce. Usually, this is because there are strict procedures and regulations to be adhered to, without room for individuals to 'do it their way'. Think of workers in a nuclear reactor or surgeons in the operating theatre.

However, think again! So long as these people are aware of all the outcomes to be achieved and they have the necessary skills and knowledge, is there not still scope for empowering them?

Procedures are stipulated because they are proven to work, but isn't it possible for workers to question procedures and identify quicker, easier or cheaper ways of achieving the desired results, or to question the desired results themselves? In cases, such as those cited above, people can be empowered to submit their ideas to the relevant parties but not to wilfully ignore procedures without necessary authorisation. We advocate creativity, not anarchy.

The **power** in em**power**ment should not be derived from authority but from brain**power**! The Armed Forces are renowned for barking out orders, yet they seek and reward initiative. Perhaps what they're really barking out are outcomes.

HOW EMPOWERMENT FITS IN

Identify the area where you
believe empowerment exists.
What are the reasons for your decision?
How does your view compare with ours
(see following pages)?

NVQs
or similar
accreditation
of the individual

ISO 9002
or TQM
(Total Quality
Management)
or other 'system'
standard

IiP
(Investors in People)
accreditation of the
organisational
culture

HOW EMPOWERMENT FITS IN

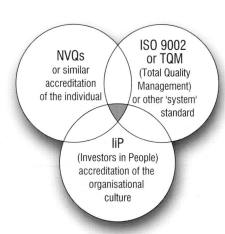

This reflects the integration of people, culture and systems, but doesn't acknowledge the ability of empowerment to find solutions or take actions where no procedure or system currently exists.

HOW EMPOWERMENT FITS IN

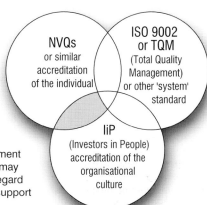

This acknowledges
that empowerment is where
an accredited or enabled workforce
is supported by the learning or development
culture of the organisation. However, it may
also suggest that it exists with total disregard
for the systems which are approved to support
the product or service.

HOW EMPOWERMENT FITS IN

NVQs
or similar
accreditation
of the individual

ISO 9002
or TQM
(Total Quality
Management)
or other 'system'
standard

IiP
(Investors in People)
accreditation of the
organisational
culture

**Empowerment
Propels!**

Empowerment cannot exist
with one initiative in isolation,
but it can exist where it has the
support of at least two initiatives at
the points where they integrate - thereby
satisfying the business needs of the organisation.

THE PARABLE OF THE SUBORDINATE

Three employees of the same organisation attended a client meeting to discuss the next phase of a project. The division manager typically took over the meeting whilst his team leader and software engineer wondered what they were doing there - they felt that things were pretty much like this back in the office.

They had travelled separately and the software engineer headed back down the motorway first whilst the other two had a one-way conversation in the car park. Several miles into the journey, the engineer encountered a major traffic jam. She was fortunate, though, in that she saw it in time to pull off at an exit.

The engineer thought of her colleagues who would be taking the same route, so she rang the team leader on her mobile phone to warn him. He was able to take an earlier exit and was grateful for the warning.

Both the team leader and the engineer thought about alerting their manager. The more they thought, the more they liked the idea of their manager getting caught up in the traffic with the ensuing frustration.

It's only human nature to react in this way. Managers do need to let go and use their human resource to optimum capacity, or suffer the consequences!

MASLOW

Most managers and students of business will have seen Abraham Maslow's 'Hierarchy of Needs' which indicates what to satisfy, and in what order, when motivating staff. In fact, Maslow identified seven innate needs, and not just the five we see in the hierarchy.

The other two innate needs exist outside the hierarchy itself because they are present all the time, at all levels.

He didn't know it at the time, but Maslow's research supports empowerment.

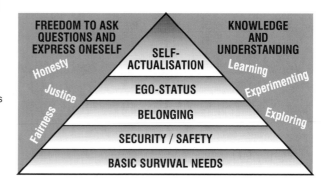

FREEDOM TO ASK QUESTIONS AND EXPRESS ONESELF

KNOWLEDGE AND UNDERSTANDING

Honesty

Justice

Fairness

Learning

Experimenting

Exploring

SELF-ACTUALISATION

EGO-STATUS

BELONGING

SECURITY / SAFETY

BASIC SURVIVAL NEEDS

MOTIVATION STYLES

Further to Maslow's theory on what motivates people, the style adopted by the motivator also has an impact on whether or not people feel empowered. There are three basic styles, but only one which is conducive to an empowerment culture:

Coercive   uses threats; breeds contempt and the possibility of sabotage; the quality of work is the bare minimum - what they can get away with

Calculative   uses rewards; breeds greed and requires you to deliver; the quality of work is acceptable - they may provide more for more reward

Co-operative   uses shared mission and information; breeds loyalty and respect, and assists empowerment; the quality of work is good to 'value-added', and provides valued opinions

Regular use of the first two styles can put an organisation into trouble; constant use of the co-operative style will instil a desire from employees to get an organisation out of trouble!

CHANGING THE LANGUAGE

What empowering people say

"My door is open if you need me"
"Will that approach meet our criteria?"
"Let's discuss your ideas"
"How can we solve this problem?"
"Ask the customers for their input"
"Thank you"

What empowered people think

I've got an idea
It's nice to feel that my contribution was
    acknowledged
What will it look like when it's done well?
Yes! I can get that sorted out for you

What directive people say

"I want to know exactly what is happening"
"That's not how I would do it. I'd ..."
"We'll do what I've suggested unless
    anyone has any objections"
"How the hell did this happen?"
"I'll tell you what they'll think, they'll think ..."
"Must I end up doing everything myself?"

What directed people think

It's about time management did something
There's no point, s/he won't listen
How do you want us to do it this time?
I need to speak to my manager

ENABLING THE INDIVIDUAL

LEADERSHIP STYLES

The situational leadership model is modified to reflect where empowering is positioned as a management style. It can only exist after enabling (coaching) has taken place and where management continues to support the employee within the agreed scope.

Enabling the individual is an important step to achieving an empowered workforce, yet it is the one most often ignored.

ENABLING   *EMPOWERING*   High in two-way involvement

DIRECTING   *DELEGATING*   Low in two-way involvement

Low in responsibility and initiative   High in responsibility and initiative

ENABLING THE INDIVIDUAL

THE TOOLKIT

As we saw in Chapter 2, empowerment is about clarifying the outcomes for people, not detailing the inputs.

However, to enable them we must provide them with the relevant toolkit. This toolkit may consist only of questions and who to ask them of, or it may contain some techniques or information which contribute in part to the overall achievement of outcomes.

The next two pages will show how, by starting at the outcomes, we can identify the appropriate tools more readily. We can show individuals how to use the tools effectively but we must not tell them how to do the job.

Enable - but don't dictate.

THE TOOLKIT

THE OUTCOME APPROACH

An OUTCOME provides an objective measure that should not be open to misinterpretation. It removes subjective assessment and indicates clearly all the significant factors that determine success.

Quite simply, the manager describes to the employees the **full** end-result they will be assessed against before they get there. Contingency and 'what if' factors should be considered at the outset. For example:

- A salesperson is required to bring in £1 million of revenue; what if it costs him £500,000 in the process?

- A programmer is tasked with setting up a particular computer program by a set date; what if another program crashes as a result?

- A driver changes a car wheel and arrives safely at his destination; what if he had left the damaged wheel at the roadside or had damaged the car in the process?

Consider all the things you consciously look for but never openly express. There should be no surprises for the empowered on what you are measuring!

THE TOOLKIT

Continuing the examples from the previous page:

The **salesperson** will still need to be given knowledge about his company's product or service, and needs training in making cold calls or appointments by telephone, overcoming objections, closing the sale, and operating within a budget. **How he puts them together is up to him** ...

The **programmer** will have been shown how to write programs using the particular language and hardware systems, and needs to understand the process from the user's viewpoint and the implications for other systems. **How she liaises and manages her time should be her prerogative** ...

The **driver** might have attended an instruction class on changing the wheel of a different car, or he might have a procedure manual to follow. **If he wants to get someone else to do the job, or to follow a different procedure, that's his choice** ...

... **so long as the outcomes are achieved**.

KEEPING CONTROL?

Control is not what we should seek if we are truly empowering. We can continue to steer by clarifying the factors for success, but we should not be trying to do the job for them.

It is still possible though to empower **and** provide direction.

COMMUNICATION

The single biggest cause of problems at work can be put down to communication, or rather a lack of it. Empowerment cannot work without effective communication at the heart of it, so it is definitely an aspect for which management and employees will need to be enabled.

Communication can be defined as:

Giving and receiving information ...

> So that ...

>> It is known to be understood ...

>>> And interpreted correctly.

- Without confirmation of understanding there is only transmission
- Both the **giver** and **receiver** have a duty to check for understanding and they may need training to help them communicate effectively
- **Enable them to plan what to say and what to ask**

COMMUNICATION
THE ENABLING COCKTAIL

This cocktail reflects the importance of communication in helping people to perform to the required level.

Once employees are armed with the right questions to clarify required outcomes and scope, the door to empowerment is open.

The cocktail is an excellent accompaniment to any course of training, and will provide much refreshment to any tired workplace!

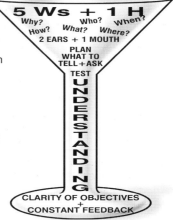

5 Ws + 1 H

Why? Who? When?
How? What? Where?
2 EARS + 1 MOUTH
PLAN
WHAT TO
TELL + ASK
TEST
UNDERSTANDING
CLARITY OF OBJECTIVES
+
CONSTANT FEEDBACK

COMMUNICATION

CASE STUDY

An Information Technology (IT) specialist was empowered to re-equip a client site with up-to-date software and hardware. He was changing the client over from WordPerfect 5.1 to Microsoft Word when two directors of the client company refused to change over. They assumed authority over him and he felt powerless to break the **impasse**. He was prepared to let them be different.

When discussing this on a workshop, we identified a key question he had not asked: 'What is it about WordPerfect that you would not be happy to lose?'

Later, once he had asked them the question, he was able to allay their fears about what they would miss and, in fact, was able to enthuse them with the features they would gain, offering one-to-one tuition in the process.

He had always possessed the power but had not been able to use it because he wasn't equipped with the right tool to take him forward, which in this case was a particular questioning technique.

DEVOLVING DECISIONS

List all the decisions, big or small, you make that affect your team or the nature of the product or service you provide:

_____

_____

_____

_____

_____

_____

Ask yourself which of these decisions could be devolved to the team. Better still, ask the team and identify with them all the relevant information they will need in order to make the most informed decision.

EMPOWERMENT GENERATES EMPOWERMENT

To empower others is to disempower yourself.

Take, for example, learning to read: once the teacher has taught you to read, she won't be needed for reading unless there is an uncertainty. She will encourage you, though, to read regularly and diversely.

However, the teacher is then available to do other things and to empower in other ways!

THE EMPOWERMENT WINDOW

This Johari-style Window shows that **empowerment** must fall ideally within the boundaries of skills, knowledge and outcomes **known** to both parties.

	KNOWN TO TEAM	NOT KNOWN TO TEAM
KNOWN TO MANAGER	EMPOWERMENT ZONE	RESTRICTED ZONE
NOT KNOWN TO MANAGER	HIDDEN POTENTIAL	UNEXPLORED

To enlarge the empowerment zone, either:

1 The manager has to enable the team, thus reducing the **restricted** zone, or

2 The team has to demonstrate further capabilities, thus reducing the **hidden potential**

The proactive solution is for the manager to adopt the role of mentor.

THE EMPOWERMENT WINDOW

Enlarging the empowerment zone can involve risk-taking ... so it's worth noting that:

- Risk also means 'accepting the chance of ...'
- 'It is easier for the losers to see what they will lose than for the gainers to see how they will gain' (Machiavelli)
- 'Men don't risk their lives for their country, they do it for medals' (Napoleon)
- Stunt teams actually take fewer risks than the average person because each stunt is expertly calculated, and each person knows exactly what is expected of them and what to expect from the others

MENTORING

An empowering manager is a <u>mentor</u>.

The British Institute of Management, in its Guide to Open Learning, states that:

'Mentoring is essentially about helping people to develop more effectively. It is a relationship designed to help build confidence and help the learner take increasing initiative for their own development'.

The word derives from Greek mythology where Mentor was a wise counsellor and an important figure in the development of Odysseus's son.

The role of mentor can be devolved to members of the team or to influential parties outside the team.

CHANGING PERCEPTIONS

This may be how many managers see their employees - unempowerable!

Undependable
Untrustworthy
Uncommitted
Incapable
Shirker
Lazy

If these same managers looked more closely they may see what these people are accomplishing outside work - far more because work itself doesn't provide what their other activities do!

Committee member
Events organiser
Voluntary worker
Club treasurer
Team manager
Instructor
Fund-raiser
Club captain

IDENTIFYING THE CONTENT

Let's return to the analogy of the driver's licence. Before the licence is granted, we will have undergone some essential driving instruction and then proved ourselves capable to an examiner on the open road.

Why then should empowerment be any different? Perhaps the difficulty is in identifying the content of the instruction and the nature of the 'test'. In the case of the driver's licence, the content might include:

- The ability to read a licence plate at 50 metres
- Moving the vehicle safely into traffic and manoeuvring through a designated course
- Proper use of the rear-view mirror and the ability to look down side-roads
- Effecting an emergency stop
- Knowledge of the Highway Code

What is it that your people should be capable of?

ENABLING THE INDIVIDUAL

IDENTIFYING THE CONTENT

List below what capabilities your people should show before you empower them:

_____

_____

_____

_____

_____

_____

_____

_____

_____

How are you going to assess their capability and how would you enable them?

CORE CONTENT

Some essentials which people may have to demonstrate before being empowered:

- The ability to ask open questions to gather all relevant facts

- Listening skills which reflect high retention of input

- The confidence to clarify their own understanding and the understanding of others

- Clarity and conciseness of written and oral communication to avoid misunderstandings

- Management of their time so that priorities are properly addressed and agreed deadlines are met

- The ability to structure a case for influencing others to take a particular course of action

4 STAGES OF LEARNING

Empowering others is like learning to drive a car!

1. **Unconsciously unskilled**: back-seat drivers. We don't know how good or bad we are because we haven't tried it for ourselves.

   - The empowerer and empowered person do not know the lines of communication and each other's skills.

2. **Consciously unskilled**: driving lesson no.1. Sitting in the car for the first time, starting the car and moving in traffic, you are aware that it's not as easy as it looks.

   - The empowerer must carefully explain the 'why' and the 'how' so that the empowered person is clear and focused and knows when to stop!

4 STAGES OF LEARNING

3. **Consciously skilled**: the driving test. When you are ready to take your test you know the Highway Code and have practised how to drive, making a conscious effort to look down side-roads and into the rear-view mirror.

   - The empowered person has been given the opportunity to try things out and has learned along the way to do new tasks, has solved new customer requirements without referral and has come up with new ideas for the team.

4. **Unconsciously skilled**: emergency stop after you have taken the test - you control the car and brake instinctively. You can drive safely without having to think so hard about it.

   - The empowered person thinks for her/himself!

IMPLEMENTING IN THE ORGANISATION

DEFINITION

By implementing we mean putting into place the requirements for the empowerment culture to be sustained and maintained.

In particular, it needs to instil trust, instil respect and generate open communication.

IMPLEMENTING IN THE ORGANISATION

GETTING EMPOWERMENT IN PLACE

1. Identify and agree the current situation.
2. Show how empowerment can improve your organisation.
3. Define the empowerment vision internally.
4. Conduct workshops to share the vision.
5. Listen to the responses and act upon them!
6. Provide mentors and encourage managers to give time to their team.
7. Provide the skills required.
8. Review appraisal system so organisations and individuals can focus on measurable achievements.
9. Review behaviour and process outcomes to keep empowerment alive.

Each of these stages is explained in detail on the following pages.

GETTING EMPOWERMENT IN PLACE

1. Identify and agree the current situation

- Define the reason for change
- Analyse where the organisation is currently
- Determine the future aim/goal/vision
- Plan the change, asking the following questions:
  - What will drive the change?
  - Who will be the custodian of the empowerment vision to ensure it becomes part of the culture?
  - How will the empowerment message be communicated?
  - What personal and organisational changes are required?
  - What is the ultimate goal of empowerment?

GETTING EMPOWERMENT IN PLACE

2. Show how empowerment can improve your organisation

- Explore the benefits in terms of increased sales, productivity and profitability from:
    - Increased commitment from staff
    - More creativity and innovation
    - Less sickness and absenteeism
    - More self-motivation
    - Better customer relations
- Use internal (staff satisfaction) surveys and customer questionnaires to identify the changes needed
- Establish benchmarks with other companies by making visits and trading information

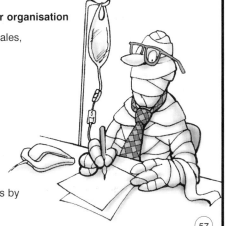

GETTING EMPOWERMENT IN PLACE

STAFF SATISFACTION SURVEYS

Staff satisfaction surveys should be viewed like a 'snapshot' of how the company is feeling. Perception matters ... because perception is reality for the individual being empowered. Survey questions should include:

- How well does your team leader communicate with you?
- Do you have a team briefing once a month?
- When did you last receive an appraisal of your work?
- How long did your appraisal last?
- When you attended your last development/technical training programme were your learning objectives discussed before and after attendance?
- Who is accountable for the part of the company in which you work?
- How do you interpret the company mission statement?
- Do you feel there is the opportunity for regular achievement at work?

Surveys should be repeated every six months.

GETTING EMPOWERMENT IN PLACE

3. Define the empowerment vision internally

Empowering your staff is ...

- When you work together to define more broadly the scope and conditions selectively and individually!
- When you give a licence to people directly or indirectly
- When the licence can be re-negotiated with the licensee, expanded or extended depending upon the situation
- Questioning assumptions you have made about the team
- When everyone knows what others are working towards and communicating this so that they are not in each other's way!

Therefore, give the right licence to the right person so that they can grow!

GETTING EMPOWERMENT IN PLACE

4. Conduct workshops to share the vision

- Participants define empowerment

- Provide the definition from page 5 - licence, enabler of results through others

- Ask delegates how empowered they feel: are they empowered to question, chase, listen, take action without referral or aim for practical solutions?

- Encourage clear communication, with guidelines on planning what to tell and what to ask

- Review by describing behaviour required - only what we see, hear and feel, not our opinions!

- Clarify the objectives we set - SMART (see page 85)

- Summarise corporate definition of Empowerment & Action plans

- Ensure all the company attends, particularly the implementers of the new culture

GETTING EMPOWERMENT IN PLACE

5. Listen to the responses and act upon them!

- Negotiate with people concerning what they will do, what they will not do and ask them what they require you to do

- Follow up action plans within a specified period

- Give credit where it is due, to the innovator or those who take action; do this at appraisal, in team briefings and in day-to-day discussions

GETTING EMPOWERMENT IN PLACE

6. Provide mentors and encourage managers to give time to their team

- Refer to the mentor definition on page 46; identify and prepare your mentors
- Establish the criteria for each relationship between mentor and mentored
- Both parties must see the benefits - what's in it for me? (W.I.I.F.M.)
- Provide a confidential contract between both parties
- Provide coaching and counselling training

GETTING EMPOWERMENT IN PLACE

HOW TO IDENTIFY MENTORS

Look for:

- Good listeners
- Those whose career has plateaued but who wish to grow the job they have
- Those who provide a listening ear in their life outside work (see page 47)
- Those who enjoy training, whether technical or personal skills
- Those with the potential for management
- Good questioners

GETTING EMPOWERMENT IN PLACE
HOW TO DEVELOP MENTORS

Selection

Firstly, learners should select a mentor who is not necessarily their own line manager. It should be someone they get on with, someone who is known as a good listener and who they respect!

Skills workshop

Enable the mentors by conducting a programme for them that should address:
- The need for mentoring and what the job will entail
- The benefits of mentoring and why the mentor will benefit, eg: extra money, skills development, etc
- What the problems will be, eg: time and frequency of help required
- Questioning and listening skills (counselling, coaching, objective feedback)
- How the system will work and who owns the system; this should include the structure of the first meeting between mentor and learner, regular reviews and the support mechanism from H.R. function (owner of the mentoring process)

GETTING EMPOWERMENT IN PLACE

THE BENEFITS OF MENTORS

Mentors can:

- Challenge, stimulate empowerment

- Identify real development opportunities that are business focused

- Act as a role-model and steer through organisational politics rather than work around them

Being a mentor should be seen as a career reward or prestigious move for the individual doing the mentoring.

GETTING EMPOWERMENT IN PLACE

7. Provide the skills required

- Provide feedback, coaching, questioning, listening, problem-solving and technical skills to allow people to grow further in their job
- Empower all the team to ask a lot of questions; they and you should accept questions as a sign of interest
- Encourage the use of **TED**, eg:

  Tell me why you need this

  Explain the processes to me and how they can be improved

  Describe to me who your customers are

Communication is the key, so help people to communicate.

GETTING EMPOWERMENT IN PLACE

8. Review the appraisal system so organisations and individuals can focus on measurable achievements

The appraisal system should have:

- The opportunity for on-going input from all people for whom the appraisee has achieved outcomes
- Self-assessment as a basis for discussion
- Assessment against previously agreed indicators of desirable performance
- Only two levels of assessment grading:
  - Achieved desired performance
  - Not achieved desired performance
- The reasons for non-achievement and how they can be remedied
- Agreed outcomes for the next review period and a personal development plan

GETTING EMPOWERMENT IN PLACE

TEAM REVIEWS

Making appraisals work can also involve regular reviews with teams to see what issues need addressing to enhance performance. Questions to ask the team:

- What are we currently doing that could be improved?
- What feedback from customers have we had recently?
- How have the changes we made last time improved/worsened the situation? (Use examples/data to support the contention)
- Where are the blockages between us and the customer?
- How can we alter the current situation?
- When will the changes be introduced?
- Who can help me to improve my knowledge of ...?

GETTING EMPOWERMENT IN PLACE

9. Review behaviour and process outcomes to keep empowerment alive

- Make it clear that everyone is responsible for keeping the empowerment fires burning in your organisation

   Like the native Indians of North America who post a person to look after the fire and tell others if the embers are dying, so too with empowerment: you need custodians to promote good practice and spot areas where more fuel or effort is required

- Publicise cases where empowerment has been successful so that people are reminded of what it looks like and that it works

GETTING EMPOWERMENT IN PLACE

SUPPORTING THE CUSTODIANS OF EMPOWERMENT

Research already tells us that within each team every individual is different and therefore the custodians that we put in place to ensure the living of empowerment may behave differently. Below, we use Belbin team styles to define the custodian's differing styles of implementing empowerment:

Co-ordinator	Clarifies goals and promotes decision-making but could delegate the 'walking of the talk'
Shaper	Challenging, will drive through change; however, will expect everyone to change behaviour immediately
Implementer	Will turn ideas into practical actions but may be inflexible about empowered outcomes created by others
Plant	Will be creative and unorthodox in approach but may ignore how the key vision will be communicated effectively
Resource Investigator	Will find out how other organisations make it work but will tend to lose enthusiasm once initial interest has passed

GETTING EMPOWERMENT IN PLACE

SUPPORTING THE CUSTODIANS OF EMPOWERMENT(Cont'd)

Team worker   Will diplomatically broach empowerment but may not see the culture change through

Monitor Evaluator   Will see all the options and be strategic but may lack the drive to inspire others

Completer Finisher   Will want the culture change delivered on time but will want to do it independently and will worry unduly about the outcomes

However, at the strategic level of an organisation Belbin says you will mostly find **Shaper and Co-ordinator** team styles. Both styles are contrasted on the following two pages.

(Acknowledgement to 'Management Teams - Why they succeed or fail', written by Professor M. Belbin, published by Heinemann)

GETTING EMPOWERMENT IN PLACE

THE CUSTODIANS OF EMPOWERMENT IN ACTION

Most managers fall into the **Shaper** or the **Co-ordinator** styles of Belbin's team roles because, perhaps, they typify the choice between being 'task' focused or 'people' focused. So, which is more conducive to empowerment?

1. The Dis-empowering Shaper:

- Will expect change in others' behaviour instantly

- Will challenge the status quo

- Will want to impose the new culture

- Will drive the culture change through the organisation but may want own vision of empowerment to prevail

- Will provoke thought throughout the organisation but may not listen to all the opinions of others let alone take heed of them

GETTING EMPOWERMENT IN PLACE

THE CUSTODIANS OF EMPOWERMENT IN ACTION (Cont'd)

2. **The Empowering Co-ordinator:**

- Can be manipulative but will understand how the culture of the organisation works through key people at all levels
- Will seek to work through (and thus empower) others
- Will want to delegate the explanation of the vision to others
- Will allow some variation of interpretation of empowerment in practice

Note: The empowerer still has to make strategic decisions that cannot be made by others.

GETTING EMPOWERMENT IN PLACE

THE CUSTODIANS OF EMPOWERMENT IN ACTION (Cont'd)

The preferred style should be that of the **Co-ordinator**.

What then is the role of the co-ordinator of the vision? Answer, to **ASK MO**!

A ssess organisational performance

S et the framework for the team

K now what is going on

M ake decisions that the team cannot

O pen doors, clear the way by guidance and enabling

GETTING EMPOWERMENT IN PLACE
HOW DO I EMPOWER?

For **POWER** to be in permanent supply it must be:

P articipative (involve everyone)
O pen (to ideas and questions)
W illing to let go (let others learn from mistakes)
E nabling (opening doors, helping to clear barriers)
R esults driven (concentrated on SMART objectives - see page 85)

(See Melrose video 'The Empowering Manager' 1995)

THE DEVOLUTION OF EMPOWERMENT

The questions that should be asked at each level:			
Any **Strategy** involves	**Vision**	Which involves asking	**Why?**
Any **Tactical** decision needs a structured	**Plan**	Which means asking	**How?**
At the **Operational** level, **What**	**Action**	Needs to be put in place	**Where?** **By Whom?** **By When?**

Remember, when you ask questions you start to sell ideas to others as the question asked frames the direction you want to head towards.

When I tell, we are discussing **my** agenda. When I sell, we are discussing **our** agenda! Therefore, telling is not selling; the latter necessitates asking questions and listening and responding to the answers.

ORGANISATIONAL LEVELS

Empowerment must work at all three levels of the organisation - **STRATEGIC, TACTICAL** and **OPERATIONAL.**

STRATEGIC

- The question to keep asking is, 'Why are we doing this?'

- Make sure everyone is clear about the vision, so they see what it will look like when empowerment helps the organisation achieve its mission

- Take care with Belbin team style **Shaper** managers who will, unreasonably, expect employees to become empowered overnight (see Custodians in this chapter)

- Ensure the process is taken slowly and deliberately; it must not be a fad but a culture change, which must endure business demands and stress, eg: no blame culture

ORGANISATIONAL LEVELS
MAINTAINING THE STRATEGY

Take the example of the railway company whose
mission was to provide enough trains for the
passenger service timetable. It decided to cut
costs and dismissed too many drivers which
resulted in many trains having to be cancelled
and caused a severe disruption to the timetable.
Passengers were not amused!

The company had lost sight of its original mission
and focused too much on cutting costs instead.
Never let the means to an end become the end in itself!

ORGANISATIONAL LEVELS

TACTICAL

The questions to ask all the time are:

- How are we going to do it?
- How will it look when we are empowering and when we are empowered?

  This must be explained - What milestones will I see when it is happening in the plans I make?

Middle managers must hear praise for trying to devolve responsibility and must involve their staff before making decisions.

ORGANISATIONAL LEVELS

OPERATIONAL

The questions to ask are, Who? What? Where? and When?

- Who do I get support from?
- Where can I go to receive help and advice (team members, other departments, etc)
- What support will I receive if things don't go to plan?
- Who will be empowered, and with what licence?
- When will the change to empowerment take place?
- When should I notice a change in me, my team, my team leader?

ORGANISATIONAL LEVELS

All of the foregoing questions need answering in advance so that the strategic direction given is explained at team briefings, at appraisal reviews and every time a boss talks to the staff!

Characteristics you may see in a manager are listed on the next page. This forms an exercise to audit empowerment in your team and organisation.

CHARACTERISTICS OF AN EMPOWERED LEADER

EXERCISE

The brief exercise below can be a useful discussion leader with groups of managers and staff alike:

❶ Which of the characteristics listed below best describes an empowered leader?

❷ On the page opposite, rank characteristics in order of priority.

❸ Once you have done this, compare your ranking with those of your team and agree a team ranking.

Leadership Characteristics

- Provides vision
- Motivates
- Respects and trusts others
- Forms good working relationships
- Has strong inter-personal skills
- Acts as a coach and mentor

- Clarifies objectives
- Sees the customer as most important
- Describes behaviour in feedback
- Devolves responsibility
- Stimulates as a mentor

CHARACTERISTICS OF AN EMPOWERED LEADER

EXERCISE

Your Ranking	Team Ranking
1 _____	_____
2 _____	_____
3 _____	_____
4 _____	_____
5 _____	_____
6 _____	_____
7 _____	_____
8 _____	_____
9 _____	_____
10 _____	_____
11 _____	_____

4 What difference would it make to your ranking if you were empowering as a leader rather than being empowered from above?

CHARACTERISTICS OF AN EMPOWERED LEADER

When the exercise described on the previous pages was used by the authors with 100 team leaders, from the perspective of being empowered, the top two rankings were consistently:

1. Clarifies objectives
The need for SMART objectives. When and what does the internal or external customer expect?

2. Respects others
Leaves decisions and action to that person, without meddling!

You might think that the characteristics **'provides vision'** and **'sees the customer as most important'** would be paramount but not according to our team leaders. They felt that there was already too much focus on creating the external image without the necessary attention internally.

CHARACTERISTICS OF AN EMPOWERED LEADER

1. CLARIFY OBJECTIVES

Be a **SMART** empowerer! Objectives must fulfil all the components of this acronym:

S pecific   the activity to which the objective relates is clearly defined

M easurable   outcomes sought which can be seen when the job is completed

A chievable   the entire job is physically possible though challenging

R ewarding   benefits the organisation, team or individual

T imebound   deadline for completion

Remember, if you haven't described the outcomes you will measure against, then you haven't done your job properly.

CHARACTERISTICS OF AN EMPOWERED LEADER

2. RESPECTING OTHERS

RESPECT the empowered!

R espect — from customers comes through application of targeted product and service knowledge

E quality — of both empowered and empowerer, eg: opening doors

S ecurity — empowerer is there to deal with big obstacles

P arameters — clearly defined according to the abilities of the individual

E mpathy — put yourself in their shoes

C ourtesy — when asking questions and giving quality time to listen

T rust — there is only one way to trust and that is to JUST DO IT; you will know from the evidence of what is said, seen and acted upon that the agreed outcomes are being achieved

TAKING ACTION

Actions speak louder than words!

- Be ruthless with your financial and material resources.

- Let your team know that you will empower but in proportion to each team member's ability and the amount each asks for.

- Err on the side of generosity. Be honest as you empower so that the team members know they need to support each other as they will all have doubts!

TAKING ACTION

ACTIONS THE ORGANISATION CAN TAKE

- Meetings: ensure that meetings have positive labels. Labels like 'post-mortem', 'defect reviews', etc, must be banned from the vocabulary! If this negative wording is publicly criticised by management, then empowerment can flourish. If empowered staff are allowed to learn from their experiences then this openness will beget more openness, up and down the organisation.

- At meetings use exception reports and action notes of key points (see next page) only to encourage debate, sharing of experiences and action to be taken. This will prevent blame being attributed and retribution exacted!

- Allow everyone in the organisation access to mainframes and even networked systems; the only exceptions should be those files holding confidential personnel information and commercial secrets.

- Hold staff development programmes that encourage open debate and are supported both during and afterwards by those with ultimate accountability.

IMPLEMENTING IN THE ORGANISATION

TAKING ACTION

ACTIONS THE ORGANISATION CAN TAKE (Cont'd)

ACTION MINUTES			
DATE OF MEETING:	**MEETING SUBJECT:**		
No.	ACTIVITY TO BE CARRIED OUT	RESPONSIBILITY	DATE REQUIRED
DATE OF NEXT MEETING:		LOCATION:	

TAKING ACTION

ACTIONS THE ORGANISATION CAN TAKE (Cont'd)

- Set projects at staff development programmes to encourage everyone to try out new ideas. These are assigned to a mentor who champions the ideas set out in the project and encourages follow up.

- Encourage empowered decisions and innovation by mentioning the ideas in company newsletters, meetings, etc, and by explaining the benefits that have accrued to the organisation.

- Develop team ownership and rewards by allocating part of the remuneration package to the achievement of departmental/team targets (eg: attainment of sales goals or service levels) though it should be noted that empowerment should be the reward in itself.

MONITORING & FEEDBACK

DEFINITION

Monitoring is: Knowing where to look and what signs to look for that empowerment is in place

Feedback is: How to communicate the successes and development needs throughout the organisation and to keep on doing so

'Feedback is food for thought and stimulus for action!' (Applegarth & Posner)

We should be looking for evidence of people being **spurred** by empowerment or **spurned** by unempowerment or disempowerment.

MONITORING & FEEDBACK

SPUR NOT SPURN

The 10 Commandments to <u>Spur</u> your workforce are:

1   Seek ideas and contributions from the team
2   Devolve decisions, from small ones to large ones
3   Involve the team in the planning stage
4   Mentor and guide but don't dictate
5   Give credit and praise for individual and group contributions
6   Focus on achievement of results (outcomes) but consider the process
7   Provide training and coaching on relevant issues
8   Allow risks and help people learn from their experiences
9   Get to know each team member, their strengths and areas for development
10 Be open with information that affects the team

Gather evidence from the workforce that these things are happening, assess the changes in productivity, effectiveness and morale, and share this information throughout the organisation so it acts as a spur.

SPUR NOT SPURN

The 10 Admonishments to <u>Spurn</u> your team are:

1   Use them like machines to do your bidding
2   Make all the decisions for them, including the small ones
3   Assign tasks rather than outcomes
4   Don't praise them when they do what they're paid for anyway
5   Let them know when they've 'failed' to do it the way you would have done it
6   Don't get familiar with them in case they take advantage
7   Be secretive, don't let them know what's going on
8   Avoid training or developing them in case they leave for a better job
9   Make sure every working minute is accounted for on timesheets
10 Show them who's boss!

Identify where these things are happening and provide support training or coaching to help the manager to 'let go'. Explore with them how each admonishment can be overcome with a spur put in its place.

BE **OPEN** TO FEEDBACK

O pen thinking
- encourage innovation in meetings and thinking outside the box

P ersonal impact
- concentrate on actions not opinions

E mpowering
- coaching, mentoring and developing are good for business

N etworking
- encourage influence and informal links across team boundaries with suppliers, customers and competitors

COMMUNICATION

An empowered organisation will establish a strong chain of communication through the **ABC**:

A ccuracy   ensure any information is accurate

B revity   ensure it is as concise as possible and promotes the vision of the company

C larity   ensure there is no ambiguity of the role you require of a team or individual, and that resources are directed to achieve empowerment

COMMUNICATION

Empowered organisations should have:

- **Two big eyes** to see opportunities and to provide descriptive feedback

- **Two big ears** to listen and describe what has been said

- **A big mouth** to communicate loudly and effectively at prescribed times when people will listen (team briefing)

> The organisation which will evolve into the next era will be slim, strong, and have a big mouth but even bigger ears

FOUR KEY MEASURES

There are four key measures used in an organisation: **Time**, **Cost**, **Quality** and **Quantity**. Of these only one looks at outcomes and allows empowerment to exist constructively. To illustrate this, let's take the example of a mail order company that sends goods to a customer:

Quantity measures inputs and outputs but only tells you how many items were sent.

Time measures tell you how long it took to make and how long to arrive.

Cost measures tell you how valuable the item is to the organisation.

Quality measures provide outcomes for the organisation as they tell you how satisfied the customer is with the goods and whether that person will purchase from your organisation again. If an earlier delivery in the day is requested by the customer and an employee is able to change the company procedure, then that is empowerment!

EMPOWERMENT INFRASTRUCTURE

An empowered organisation encourages the entire company to believe in empowerment and checks to see that the 'infrastructure' for empowerment is in place.

- All work, both paper-based and information systems, must be allocated according to client/customer and not discipline.

- Offices are resources which can be booked out to anyone - they are not status symbols. They are used between meetings for communicating, writing and reading.

- There should be sharing of resources - no personal desk space, lockers, shoulder bags, laptops, etc (adopt a booking system for resources).

99

EMPOWERMENT INFRASTRUCTURE

The empowered organisation will check that:

- Conversation takes place in the corridors and other common areas, instead of always in full-blown meetings which are costly in terms of time and missed opportunities (ie: the opportunities afforded by impromptu meetings).

- A separate room is allocated for each major client, where one team works on that particular client assignment.

- The car park layout does not reserve spaces for senior managers and executives - only for those customers/suppliers visiting the company.

- The external infrastructure - pathways, benches, trees, lawns and flowers - is conducive to productive conversation.

EMPOWERMENT INFRASTRUCTURE

The empowered organisation ensures that there are adequate refreshment areas
(eg: restaurant, canteens, coffee areas) and break times. In these cost-conscious days
many organisations regard these as wasteful.

What do people do when they take a break?

- They refresh their minds and thereby reduce stress levels.

- They also enjoy the company of others working towards a similar cause.

- Network with other team members, departments and all levels of the organisation.
  Each communicates with the other and receives feedback!

- Unwind and find time away from the desk in which to have new ideas!

THE DRIPPING TAP

Feedback should be like a dripping tap; rather than turning the water full on or off at appraisal time, give feedback to your team members - a little and often (in small drips).

Keep empowerment going at appraisals and team briefings by giving descriptive feedback. Describe what you saw, heard and felt. This will de-personalise and reduce any tension. Do not save it up until appraisal time.

Thus there are no surprises and the empowered person grows in confidence to take action and grows in his or her own job every day!

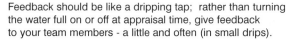

THE ACID TEST

Ask any member of the organisation to define empowerment. Then ask the same person to describe delegation and then compare the difference.

Our knowledge of organisations tells us that often empowerment is seen as the same as delegation. If you find this then you need to go back and start the process again!

If the organisation is still talking about empowerment then it has not yet achieved an empowered workforce! When empowered actions go unremarked, then empowerment is present because it has been accepted as the norm!

Feedback from the team is all about being spurred and not spurned!

CONCLUSION

Clearly, you **empower** when you allow all members of the team:

- Licence to think!
- Licence to plan!
- Licence to act!

BIBLIOGRAPHY / REFERENCES

'Management Teams: Why They Succeed or Fail', Meredith Belbin, Heinemann

'Zapp: The Lightning of Empowerment', William C. Byham, Century Business

'Empowerment: Building A Committed Workforce', Cynthia D. Scott and Dennis T. Jaffe, Kogan Page

'Guide to Open Learning', British Institute of Management

'The Empowering Manager', Melrose Film Productions

About the Authors

Mike Applegarth has been a training professional for nearly twenty years, fifteen of them spent as a consultant. His assignments have involved him in a range of industries from insurance to petrochemicals, and his clients are within both the private and public sectors, and amongst charitable institutions.

He specialises in aspects of communication and team-building, whether it be for office staff, management or sales personnel, and has been actively involved with the development and application of competence-based performance standards within the National Vocational Qualification (NVQ) framework. Each training solution is individually tailored and can take the form of a delivered programme or distance-learning material.

He is the author of 'How To Take A Training Audit', first printed in July 1991 as a leader in the Kogan Page Practical Trainer series. It reflects the breadth of his training expertise, whilst his versatility is supported by other, client workbooks which include: 'An Introduction to Insurance', 'Boiler-house Theory', and 'Automotive Lubricants and Hydraulic Oils'.

Mike can be contacted at: Applegarth Professional Training, Lawnswood House, Goldhill, Lower Bourne, Farnham, Surrey GU10 3JH   Telephone & Fax: (01252) 733044

About the Authors

Keith Posner was professionally trained by Nationwide Building Society before joining Cornhill Insurance as Assistant Training Manager in 1991. Before leaving Cornhill in 1995 he finished managing the specialist training function on the Business Process Review project team. This encompassed planning and implementing the training of 200 Customer Service Advisors across thirteen UK branches, as well as delivering BPR programmes.

Keith employed Mike Applegarth as a consultant at Cornhill, and in 1995-96 they worked together on a management development assignment for one of Mike's clients involved in information technology outsourcing. This was where their approach to empowerment was first formulated.

Keith also operates independently, specialising in coaching, stress management and team-building. He is a licensed user and tester in the use of Occupational Personality Questionnaires and a licensed Trained Trainer in the Continuous Improvement Programme.

Keith can be contacted at: Positive Perspective, The Coach House, Henfold Lane, South Holmwood, Dorking, Surrey RH5 4NX
(Tel: 01306 888990).

ORDER FORM

Your details

Name _____

Position _____

Company _____

Address _____

_____

_____

Telephone _____

Facsimile _____

E-mail _____

VAT No. (EC companies) _____

Your Order Ref _____

Please send me:

		No. copies
The Empowerment	Pocketbook	
The _____	Pocketbook	
The _____	Pocketbook	
The _____	Pocketbook	
The _____	Pocketbook	

Order by Post

MANAGEMENT POCKETBOOKS LTD
14 EAST STREET ALRESFORD HAMPSHIRE SO24 9EE UK

Order by Phone, Fax or Internet

Telephone: +44 (0)1962 735573
Facsimile: +44 (0)1962 733637
E-mail: pocketbks@aol.com
Web: www.pocketbook.co.uk

Customers in USA should contact:
Stylus Publishing, LLC, 22883 Quicksilver Drive, Sterling, VA 20166-2012
Telephone: 703 661 1581 or 800 232 0223
Facsimile: 703 661 1501 E-mail: styluspub@aol.com

THE MANAGEMENT POCKETBOOK SERIES

Pocketbooks

Appraisals Pocketbook
Assertiveness Pocketbook
Balance Sheet Pocketbook
Business Planning Pocketbook
Business Presenter's Pocketbook
Business Writing Pocketbook
Challengers Pocketbook
Coaching Pocketbook
Communicator's Pocketbook
Creative Manager's Pocketbook
Cross-cultural Business Pocketbook
Cultural Gaffes Pocketbook
Customer Service Pocketbook
Empowerment Pocketbook
Export Pocketbook
Facilitator's Pocketbook
Improving Profitability Pocketbook
Interviewer's Pocketbook
Key Account Manager's Pocketbook
Learner's Pocketbook

Managing Budgets Pocketbook
Managing Cashflow Pocketbook
Managing Change Pocketbook
Managing Your Appraisal Pocketbook
Manager's Pocketbook
Manager's Training Pocketbook
Marketing Pocketbook
Meetings Pocketbook
Mentoring Pocketbook
Motivation Pocketbook
Negotiator's Pocketbook
People Manager's Pocketbook
Performance Management Pocketbook
Personal Success Pocketbook
Problem Behaviour Pocketbook
Project Management Pocketbook
Quality Pocketbook
Sales Excellence Pocketbook
Salesperson's Pocketbook
Self-managed Development Pocketbook
Stress Pocketbook

Teamworking Pocketbook
Telephone Skills Pocketbook
Telesales Pocketbook
Thinker's Pocketbook
Time Management Pocketbook
Trainer Standards Pocketbook
Trainer's Pocketbook

Pocketfiles/Other

Leadership: Sharing The Passion
The Great Presentation Scandal
Trainer's Blue Pocketfile of
Ready-to-use Exercises
Trainer's Green Pocketfile of
Ready-to-use Exercises
Trainer's Red Pocketfile of
Ready-to-use Exercises

Audio Cassettes

Tips for Presenters
Tips for Trainers

Published by:
Management Pocketbooks Ltd
14 East Street, Alresford, Hants SO24 9EE, U.K.
Tel: +44 (0)1962 735573   Fax: +44 (0)1962 733637
E-mail: pocketbks@aol.com
Web: www.pocketbook.co.uk

All rights reserved.

First published 1997. Reprinted 1999

© Mike Applegarth and Keith Posner 1997

ISBN: 1 870471 51 2

British Library Cataloguing-in-Publication Data – A catalogue record for this book
is available from the British Library.

Printed in U.K.